LOCOMOTIVES &
OF BORD na MÓ

Stephen Johnson

Midland Publishing Limited

Locomotives and Railcars of Bord na Móna
© 1996, Stephen M Johnson
ISBN 1 85780 045 1

Design concept and layout
© Midland Publishing Limited

Published in 1996 by
Midland Publishing Limited
24 The Hollow, Earl Shilton, Leicester,
LE9 7NA, England
Tel: +44 (0)1455 847815
Fax: +44 (0)1455 841805

Printed in England
by Clearpoint Colourprint Limited
Daybrook, Nottingham, NG5 6HD

Acknowledgements:
All photographs are by Stephen Johnson unless
otherwise acknowledged.
The author is grateful for assistance from
the following individuals and organisations,
during the preparation of this book:
Cavan & Leitrim Railway, Dave Holroyd,
Robert Darvill (Industrial Railway Society),
Narrow Gauge Railway Society,
Peter Nicholson, Hamish Stevenson.

Front cover photo: *Hunslet diesel-hydraulic LM380
hauls a rake of wagons under the Dublin-Cork main line
at Coolnamona, while an Iarnród Éireann 201 class
passes overhead, on 4th August 1996.*

Inside front cover, top: *The final Hunslet type heads
a rake of wagons away from Lanesborough Power
Station on 31st July 1995.*

Inside front cover, bottom: *F321, one of the Bord's rail
tractors, clearly showing its Massey Ferguson origins,
stands in the yard at Boora Works on 3rd August 1995.*

Title page: *A Ruston 40DL heads a rake of wagons
being loaded with milled Peat.* Midland Publishing
Limited collection

Inside back cover, top: *Ruston & Hornsby 40DL LM171
stands in the yard at Boora Works on 3rd August 1995.*

Inside back cover, bottom: *Bord na Móna railcar C80
at Blackwater on 2nd August 1995.*

Back cover, top: *LM228 crosses the swing-bridge
across the grand canal with a rake of wagons bound for
Lemanaghan on 3rd August 1995.*

Back cover, bottom: *LM323 heads the Clonmacnoise &
West Offaly train at Blackwater on 25th July 1994.*

Below: *Ruston & Hornsby 40DL LM170 at Templetouhy,
County Tipperary, on 12th July 1973.* Peter Nicholson

Introduction

Bord na Móna, or Irish Peat Commission, is a semi-state body formed in 1946 to develop the peat reserves of the Republic, to best advantage. Upon its formation, the Bord acquired bogs worked previously by the Turf Development Board at Glenties, Clonsast and Lullymore.

The business of the Bord may be divided into three distinct areas, the Peat Energy Division, the Horticultural Division and Home Fuels Division. The largest, Peat Energy, concentrates on producing milled peat for use in Bord Solathair an Leictreachais (Electricity Supply Board or ESB) power stations. The latter are concentrated in the Bog of Allen area, a vast acreage stretching from the outskirts of Dublin into County Galway.

The first power stations were fired by sod peat, that is basically chunks of peat burnt in a furnace. Wagons of sod peat were brought in from the bogs by Bord na Móna and left in reception sidings. The ESB had its own locomotives, which took a wagon at a time to the unloading point. The wagon body and its load were lifted by a crane, leaving bogies behind, hoisted to the top of the power station building and tipped into hoppers. Portarlington, Allenwood and Lanesborough 'A' had such systems. The former and latter are now closed and ESB no longer have their own locomotives. Later power stations use milled peat, a fine grain material not unlike garden peat. This is unloaded in rotary tipplers and taken by conveyor belt to the power station. The whole process is a lot quicker and wagons may be unloaded without uncoupling. Milled peat is blown into the furnace, a far more efficient way of producing electricity.

The Horticultural Division harvests peat for use in horticultural products. Milled peat is used in such products as Shamrock Moss Peat, the Bord's own brand. Other well known companies ship peat out in containers for processing and packing in England and on the Continent.

The third part of the business produces peat briquettes, a solid fuel for use in open fires as a substitute for coal. A briquette is made by compressing milled peat in a pug mill to form hand sized rectangular blocks. They are a popular fuel, a modern form of the traditional Irish turf fire..

The majority of the Bord's tracks are of the 3ft gauge, the exception being Glenties which has a 2ft gauge system. Kilberry was also a 2ft gauge stronghold, but has recently been re-gauged to 3ft. A number of 2ft gauge locomotives remain dumped at Kilberry.

The system consists of permanently laid lines connecting the main works, power stations and factories to the actual peat producing area of the bog. Temporary lines are laid from the main line to the areas currently in production, thus the total track mileage in use can vary almost daily. Blackwater for instance has some 96 miles of permanent track with up to 50 miles of temporary lines in use – and this is only one system!

Some systems have considerable lengths of double track main lines with triangular junctions, level crossings and bridges, including the impressive 595ft long Shannon Viaduct at Shannonbridge. It is estimated that there is some 1200 miles of track in use, making Bord na Móna's railway system not only larger than those of Iarnrod Éireann and Northern Ireland Railways, but the largest industrial railway in Europe, moving some 5 million tons annually.

In recent years Bord na Móna have joined up a number of bog systems. Blackwater is linked to Boora via Lemanaghan, making it possible to travel from the outskirts of Athlone (Bunnahinly Bog) to near Ballinasloe (Culliaghmore Bog) or Tullamore (Killaranny Bog). Similarly, Clonsast is now connected to Derrygreenagh at Derrycricket Bog, also at Clongreen Bog to the Ballydermot-Timahoe system. This makes a journey from outside Mountmellick (Garryhinch Bog) to near Enfield (Timahoe North Bog) possible.

Bord na Móna also run two tourist railways in the form of the Clonmacnoise & West Offaly Railway at Blackwater and the Bellacorick Bog Railway at Oweninny. Passengers can enjoy a guided tour around the bogs in the comfort of an air conditioned carriage at Blackwater or the passenger saloon of one of the railcars previously in service on CIE's now closed West Clare Railway, at Bellacorick. Both trips are well worth going on.

Finally, the railways and locomotives of Bord na Móna make for fascinating study, but it should be noted that this is a working industrial railway and written permission should always be obtained prior to any visit to an installation, as trespass is illegal and potentially dangerous.

Stephen Johnson
Warwick   July 1996

Locomotive Depot Locations

Throughout this book, reference is made to the 'Allocation' of a particular vehicle: in effect this is the location of its depot. The following list of depot allocations includes a one, two or three letter abbreviation code, which accord with those used over the years by the Industrial Railway Society. The codes have not been used in the main body of the book since there was adequate space for them to appear in full. The codes 'An' and 'Kd' which have been introduced in the following list are the author's own abbreviations.

Allen (An), County Kildare.
2 miles east of Allen on the minor road from Allen to Morristown Lattin, north of Newbridge.
Attymon (At), County Galway.
6 miles east of Athenry on the L99 road 1½ miles south of Attymon Junction Station.
Ballydermot (Bd), County Kildare.
1½ miles north of Rathangan on the R401 Kildare to Edenderry road.
Bellair (Be), County Offaly.
3 miles north of Ballycumber on the Ballycumber to Moate minor road.
Ballivor (Bi), County Westmeath.
6 miles west of Ballivor on the R156 Trim to Mullingar road.
Blackwater (Bl), County Offaly.
1½ miles east of Shannonbridge on the L27 road to Cloghan.
Bangor Erris (Bn), County Mayo.
2 miles west of Bangor off the road to Belmullet on the minor road to Srahmore.
Boora (Bo), County Offaly.
6 miles east of Cloghan on the L2 Tullamore road.
Coolnagun (Cg), County Westmeath.
5 miles west of Castlepollard off the R395 road to Granard, 2 miles south of Coole on the way to Multyfarnham.
Clonkeen (Ck), County Galway. Sub-shed of Attymon.
1½ miles west of Attymon Junction Station on the minor road to Athenry.
Coolnamona (Cm), County Laois.
3½ miles south of Portlaoise on the N8 road to Abbeyleix.
Clonsast (Cs), County Offaly.
3 miles north of Portarlington on the L26 road to Rochfortbridge. Closed.
Derryfadda (De), County Galway.
2 miles south west of Ballyforan on the Ballyforan to Kilglass minor road.
Derrygreenagh (Dg), County Offaly.
2 miles south of Rochfortbridge on L112 Rhode road.
Gilltown (Gi), County Kildare.
South of the Donadea to Timahoe Road at Derryvarroge.
Glenties (Gl), County Donegal. 2ft gauge.
2 miles south west of Glenties on N56 Ardara road.

Kilberry (K), County Kildare.
3 miles north west of Athy on the L18 Monasterevan road.
Kinnegad (Kd), County Meath
1 mile south of Kinnegad on the minor road to Ballinabrackey
Lemanaghan (Le), County Offaly.
Part of the Boora System. At Ferbane on the N62 Birr to Athlone road.
Littleton (Li), County Tipperary.
1½ miles south of Littleton on the N8, near Thurles.
Lullymore (Lu), County Kildare.
3 miles from Allenwood on the L2 Edenderry road.
Monettia (Mo), County Offaly.
2 miles south of Killeigh on the minor road to Clonaslee to the east of Gorteen Bridge
Mountdillon (M), Derryarogue, County Longford.
2 miles east of Lanesborough on the N63 to Longford.
Tionnsca Abhainn Einne (TAE), Oweninny, County Mayo. 9 miles west of Crossmolina on the N59 Belmullet road.
Templetouhy (Te), County Tipperary.
3 miles south east of Templetouhy on the L110 Templemore to Urlingford road.
Timahoe (Ti), County Kildare.
3 miles west of Prosperous on the L2 Clane to Edenderry road at the village of Corduff.
Ummeras (U), County Kildare.
4 miles north of Monasterevan on the Monasterevan to Bracknagh minor road.

Former and Closed Locations

Barna (Ba), County Cork. Closed.
10 miles south east of Castleisland, near Ballydesmond.
Carrigcannon (Ca), County Kerry. Closed.
7 miles north of Castleisland on the L9 road to Listowel.
Derryaghan (Da), County Longford. Sub-shed of Derryarogue (Mountdillon, or Clonflower).
Garryduff (Gd), Clonfert Bridge, County Offaly. Part of the Blackwater System. At Clonfert on the Banagher to Lawrencetown minor road.
Garryhinch (Gh), County Offaly. Part of the Clonsast System, 1 mile from Clonygowan off the L108 Portarlington road.
Lyracrumpane (Ly), County Kerry. Closed.
On the L9 Castleisland to Listowel road.
Mountdillon Old Works (Mw), County Roscommon. Closed. A sub-shed of Derryarogue.
Turruan (Tu), County Offaly. Part of the Boora System. 3 miles from Ferbane on the L113 Clara road.

THE BOGS OF
BORD NA MÓNA

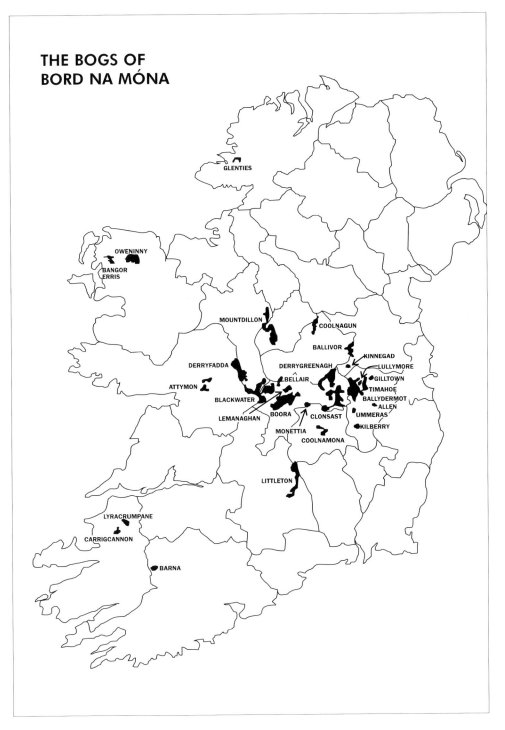

Original Numbering System

Glenties and Clonsast were the first bogs to open, around 1939. Glenties began operations with Ruston & Hornsby 200075 of 1940 (later LM16). Clonsast had the following locomotives and maintained a separate list for several years:

DIESEL OR PETROL LOCOMOTIVES

No	Type	Maker/No	Built	Remarks
1	4wDM	R&H 198251	1939	Later LM 13
2	4wDM	R&H 198290	1940	Later LM 14
3	4wDM	R&H 198326	1940	Later LM 15
4	?	HM/?	c1939	Sold/scrapped
5	4wPM	Wickham/?	?	S/s after 1953
6	4wDM	R&H 244870	1946	Later LM 24
7	4wDM	R&H 244871	1946	Later LM 25
8	4wDM	R&H 249524	1946	Later LM 27
8	4wDM	R&H 259737	1948	Later LM 59
9	4wDM	R&H 249525	1946	c1948 to ESB Portarlington as No.2
9	4wDM	R&H 329682	1952	Later LM 78
10	4wDM	R&H 249526	1946	c1947 to ESB Portarlington as No.1

STEAM LOCOMOTIVES

No	Type	Maker/No	Built	Remarks
1	0-4-0WT	AB 2263	1949	Later LM 43
2	0-4-0WT	AB 2264	1949	Later LM 44
3	0-4-0WT	AB 2265	1949	Later LM 45

Early Local Numbering

Other bogs opened later with their own local numbering systems. About 1954 these were assimilated, by date order, into a national numbering scheme in which the locomotive numbers were prefixed with 'LM', which is understood to stand for 'Locomotive Machine'.

DIESEL OR PETROL LOCOMOTIVES

No	Make/Yr	Later no	No	Make/Yr	Later no
1	R&H 1947	LM 34	1	R&H 1952	LM 83
2	R&H 1947	LM 33	2	R&H 1947	LM 36
2	Deutz 1960	LM 189	3	R&H 1947	LM 37
4	R&H 1947	LM 32	4	Deutz 1960	LM 191
5	R&H 1948	LM 66	5	R&H 1943	LM 177
6	R&H 1948	LM 71	6	R&H 1948	LM 74
6	R&H 1955	LM 137	7	R&H 1948	LM 56
7	Deutz 1960	LM 194	8	R&H 1948	LM 73
8	R&H 1954	LM 104	10	R&H 1952	LM 79
11	R&H 1947	LM 30	12	R&H 1946	LM 28
13	R&H 1952	LM 80	14	R&H 1952	LM 84
15	R&H 1948	LM 52	15	R&H 1954	LM 116
16	R&H 1952	LM 88	17	R&H 1948	LM 67
18	R&H 1941	Imported August 1973 for spares. Ex-Whittlesea Central Brick Co Ltd. Cambridgeshire. Dismantled at Lullymore, Co Kildare.			

Abbreviations used above:

AB = Andrew Barclay. R&H = Ruston & Hornsby.
HM = Hannoversche Machinenbau AG.
ESB = Electricity Supply Board.

Numerical Listings of Stock

On the following pages the locomotives, railcars and tractors are arranged in numbering scheme order and divided into blocks of manufacturers' model types, with known technical data. The vehicle number is followed by the manufacturers' works number (if any), then its last known allocation and a note if it has been either dismantled, preserved, sold, scrapped or is just out of use.

Bord na Móna also applied a single letter suffix after the locomotive number, the purpose of which is unknown. Use of this suffix was discontinued from around 1958, although some locomotives still carry these letters today.

The listing of the early locomotives acquired by the Bord is known to be incomplete. For instance, it is understood that the Bord had various Motor Rail locos and more than the single Ruhrthaler listed, but definite proof has yet to come to light.

In order to keep the locomotives working, over the years the Bord have modified a number of individual machines. Some of the early Rustons now have Gardner engines, and some of the Wagonmasters have been rebuilt with hydraulic transmission and look very different to the original. These modifications make for a very interesting fleet, to the student of industrial railways.

A recent development is that the Bord are currently building their own locomotives. Eight have been constructed so far, numbered from LM389.

Recently, a form of privatisation has been in progress and three of the Bord's bog systems are now workers co-operatives. The vehicles used on these co-operatives are summarised on page 46: their details also appear in the main lists.

LOCOMOTIVE NUMBERING SEQUENCE

RUHRTHALER

		0-4-0DM	
Built:	c.1936	Engine:	Hatz. Later replaced with a Gardner 4LW.
Weight:		Transmission:	
Wheel Diameter:		Horsepower:	
Gauge:	3 ft	Tractive Effort:	

Fleet No	Makers No	Remarks
☐ LM 11	1082	Engineless when purchased for preservation in 1973.

This loco is now at the Narrow Gauge Railway Centre, Gloddfa Ganol Slate Mine, Blaenau Ffestiniog.

WHITCOMB

		4wDM	
Built:	1945	Engine:	
Weight:		Transmission:	
Wheel Diameter:		Horsepower:	
Gauge:	3 ft	Tractive Effort:	

Fleet No	Makers No	Allocation	Remarks
☐ LM 12	40331	Kilberry	Engine replaced with a Gardner 4LW

Whitcomb 4wDM LM12 at Carrigcannon, County Kerry, in the summer of 1973. Peter Nicholson

RUSTON & HORNSBY 33/40HP

4wDM

Built:	1939, 1940†	Engine:	Ruston 3VRO
Weight:	5½ tons	Transmission:	3-speed, chain
Wheel Diameter:	1 ft 6 in	Horsepower:	40 hp at 1,200 rpm
Gauge:	3 ft	Tractive Effort:	2,950 lbs

Fleet No	Makers No	Allocation	Remarks
☐ **LM 13 D**	198251	Kilberry	
☐ **LM 14 D†**	198290	Clonsast	Out of use

RUSTON & HORNSBY 16/20HP

4wDM

Built:	1940	Engine:	Ruston 2VSO. Later replaced with a Ford.
Weight:	3¼ tons	Transmission:	3-speed, chain
Wheel Diameter:	1 ft 6 in	Horsepower:	20 hp at 1,200 rpm
Gauge:	3 ft	Tractive Effort:	

Fleet No	Makers No	Remarks
☐ **LM 15**	198326	It was privately preserved at Cahir, and subsequently scrapped

RUSTON & HORNSBY 16/20HP

4wDM

Built:	1940	Engine:	Ruston 2VSO
Weight:	3¼ tons	Transmission:	3-speed, chain
Wheel Diameter:	1 ft 6 in	Horsepower:	20 hp at 1,200 rpm
Gauge:	2 ft	Tractive Effort:	

Fleet No	Makers No	Allocation	Remarks
☐ **LM 16 B**	200075	Kilberry	Out of use

R&H 16/20hp
LM15 at Littleton,
County Tipperary,
12th July 1973.
Peter Nicholson

RUSTON & HORNSBY 48DL 4wDM

Built:	1946
Weight:	7 tons
Wheel Diameter:	1 ft 6 in
Gauge:	3 ft

Engine:	Ruston 4VRH, Gardner 4LW*
Transmission:	3-speed, twin ratio, chain
Horsepower:	48 hp at 1,200 rpm
Tractive Effort:	3,780 lbs

Fleet No	Makers No	Allocation	Remarks
☐ LM 17 E*	242901	Attymon	
☐ LM 18 G	242902	Tionnsca	

RUSTON & HORNSBY 13DL 4wDM

Built:	1946
Weight:	3 tons
Wheel Diameter:	1 ft 6 in
Gauge:	3 ft

Engine:	Ruston 2VTH
Transmission:	3-speed, chain
Horsepower:	13 hp at 1,200 rpm
Tractive Effort:	

Fleet No	Makers No	Allocation	Remarks
☐ LM 19	243386	Clonsast	Dismantled

RUSTON & HORNSBY 13DL 4wDM

Built:	1946
Weight:	3 tons
Wheel Diameter:	1 ft 6 in
Gauge:	2 ft

Engine:	Ruston 2VTH, Ford*, Deutz†
Transmission:	3-speed, chain
Horsepower:	13 hp at 1,200 rpm
Tractive Effort:	

Fleet No	Makers No	Allocation	Remarks
☐ LM 20 A*	243387	Glenties	
☐ LM 21 A†	243392	Kilberry	Out of use

2ft gauge
R&H 13DL LM21
at Kilberry,
County Kildare,
10th July 1973.
Peter Nicholson

RUSTON & HORNSBY 13DL

4wDM

Built:	1947	Engine:	Ruston 2VTH
Weight:	3 tons	Transmission:	3-speed, chain
Wheel Diameter:	1 ft 6 in	Horsepower:	13 hp at 1,200 rpm
Gauge:	3 ft	Tractive Effort:	

Fleet No	Makers No	Remarks
☐ **LM 22**	243395	Rebuilt by Bord na Móna as a 4wDMR. Sold or scrapped

RUSTON & HORNSBY 40DL

4wDM

Built:	1946	Engine:	Ruston 3VRH, Gardner 4LW*
Weight:	5½ tons	Transmission:	3-speed, chain
Wheel Diameter:	1 ft 6 in	Horsepower:	40 hp at 1,200 rpm
Gauge:	3 ft	Tractive Effort:	2,950 lbs

Fleet No	Makers No	Allocation	Remarks
☐ **LM 23 E***	244788	Clonsast	Out of use
☐ **LM 24 E**	244870	Derrygreenagh	Formerly Clonsast No 6. Out of use
☐ **LM 25 E**	244871	Clonsast	Formerly Clonsast No 7. Out of use

RUSTON & HORNSBY 40DL

4wDM

Built:	1947	Engine:	Ruston 3VRH. Later replaced with a Gardner 4LW
Weight:	5½ tons	Transmission:	3-speed, chain
Wheel Diameter:	1 ft 6 in	Horsepower:	40 hp at 1,200 rpm
Gauge:	2 ft	Tractive Effort:	2,950 lbs

Fleet No	Makers No	Allocation	Remarks
☐ **LM 26 E**	248458	Glenties	Sold or scrapped

*R&H 13DL
LM22 at Timahoe,
County Kildare,
August 1973.
Peter Nicholson*

RUSTON & HORNSBY 48DL   4wDM

Built:	1946	Engine:	Ruston 4VRH, *Gardner 4LW
Weight:	7 tons	Transmission:	3-speed, twin ratio, chain
Wheel Diameter:	1 ft 6 in	Horsepower:	40 hp at 1,200 rpm
Gauge:	3 ft	Tractive Effort:	3,780 lbs

Fleet No	Makers No	Allocation	Remarks
☐ **LM 27 G**	249524	Gilltown	Formerly No 8
☐ **LM 28 G**	249543	Timahoe	Formerly No 12
☐ **LM 29 G**	249544	Mountdillon	Scrapped
☐ **LM 30 G***	249545	Gilltown	Formerly No 11

RUSTON & HORNSBY 40DL   4wDM

Built:	1947	Engine:	Ruston 3VRH, Gardner 4LW*
Weight:	5½ tons	Transmission:	3-speed, chain
Wheel Diameter:	1 ft 6 in	Horsepower:	40 hp at 1,200 rpm
Gauge:	3 ft	Tractive Effort:	2,950 lbs

Fleet No	Makers No	Allocation	Remarks
☐ **LM 31 E**	252232	?	
☐ **LM 32 E**	252233	Timahoe	Formerly No 4
☐ **LM 33 E**	252234	?	Formerly No 2. Sold or scrapped
☐ **LM 34 E***	252239	Attymon	Formerly No 1
☐ **LM 35 E***	252240	Coolnagan	
☐ **LM 36 E**	252241	Mountdillon	Formerly No 2
☐ **LM 37 E***	252245	Mountdillon	Formerly No 3
☐ **LM 38 E***	252246	Attymon	
☐ **LM 39 E**	252247	Mountdillon	
☐ **LM 40 E**	252251	Mountdillon	
☐ **LM 41 E***	252252	Clonkeen	

*2ft gauge
R&H 20DL
LM42 (left) and
R&H 16/20HP
LM16 (right)
at Kilberry,
County Kildare,
10th July 1973.
Peter Nicholson*

RUSTON & HORNSBY 20DL   4wDM

Built:	1947	Engine:	Ruston 2VSH
Weight:	3½ tons	Transmission:	3-speed, chain
Wheel Diameter:	1 ft 4⁵⁄₁₆ in	Horsepower:	20 hp at 1,200 rpm
Gauge:	2 ft	Tractive Effort:	

Fleet No	Makers No	Allocation	Remarks
☐ **LM 42 C**	252849	Kilberry	Out of use

ANDREW BARCLAY   0-4-0WT

Built:	1949	Boiler Pressure:	180 psi
Weight:	10¼ tons	Cylinders:	8½ x 12 in
Wheel Diameter:	2 ft	Horsepower:	
Gauge:	3 ft	Tractive Effort:	5,527 lbs

Fleet No	Makers No	Remarks
☐ **LM 43**	2263	Formerly No 1. Rebuilt as No 7 *Tom Rolt* by the Talyllyn Railway
☐ **LM 44**	2264	Formerly No 2. Preserved by the Irish Steam Preservation Society at Stradbally as No 2
☐ **LM 45**	2265	Formerly No 3. Preserved at Shane's Castle as *Shane*

One of the trio of Andrew Barclay-built 0-4-0WT steam locomotives, displaying both LM43 and No.1, at Portarlington in 1964. John Edgington

RUSTON & HORNSBY 40DL — 4wDM

Built:	1948	Engine:	Ruston 3VRH, Gardner 4LW*
Weight:	5½ tons	Transmission:	3-speed, chain
Wheel Diameter:	1 ft 6 in	Horsepower:	40 hp at 1,200 rpm
Gauge:	3 ft	Tractive Effort:	2,950 lbs

Fleet No	Makers No	Allocation	Remarks
☐ LM 46	259184	Ballydermot	
☐ LM 47 F	259185	Kilberry	
☐ LM 48 F*	259186	Ballydermot	
☐ LM 49 F*	259189	Tionnsca	
☐ LM 50*	259190	Coolnagun	
☐ LM 51 F*	259191	Coolnagun	
☐ LM 52 F	259196	Kilberry	Formerly No 15
☐ LM 53 F	259197	Ballydermot	
☐ LM 54 F*	259198	Kilberry	
☐ LM 55 F*	259205	Ballydermot	
☐ LM 56 F	259204	Gilltown	Formerly No 7
☐ LM 57 F	259203	Gilltown	
☐ LM 58 F*	259206	Littleton	
☐ LM 59	259737	Clonsast	Out of use
☐ LM 60 F*	259738	Derrygreenagh	
☐ LM 61 F	259739	Ballivor	Dismantled
☐ LM 62 F*	259743	Ballivor	
☐ LM 63 F*	259744	Ballivor	
☐ LM 64 F	259745	Clonsast	Out of use
☐ LM 65*	259749	Littleton	
☐ LM 66	259750	Mountdillon	Formerly No 5
☐ LM 67 F	259751	Timahoe	Formerly No 17
☐ LM 68*	259752	Littleton	
☐ LM 69 F*	259755	Ballivor	
☐ LM 70 F*	259756	Coolnagun	
☐ LM 71 F	259757	Mountdillon	Formerly No 6
☐ LM 72 F*	259758	Mountdillon	
☐ LM 73	259759	Mountdillon	Formerly No 8
☐ LM 74 F	259760	Ballydermot	Formerly No 6

*R&H 40DL
LM52 at Timahoe,
County Kildare,
19th July 1973.
Its former number
'15' is just visible
below the cab-
side window.
Peter Nicholson*

R&H 40DL
LM59 at the
refuelling point at
Garryhinch,
County Offaly,
10th July 1973.
Peter Nicholson

RUSTON & HORNSBY 48DL

4wDM

Built:	1952	Engine:	Ruston 4VRH
Weight:	7 tons	Transmission:	3-speed, twin ratio, chain
Wheel Diameter:	1 ft 6 in	Horsepower:	48 hp at 1,200 rpm
Gauge:	3 ft	Tractive Effort:	3,780 lbs

Fleet No	Makers No	Allocation	Remarks
☐ **LM 75 R**	326047	Lullymore	Out of use
☐ **LM 76**	326048	Bellair	

RUSTON & HORNSBY 40DL

4wDM

Built:	1952, 1954†	Engine:	Ruston 3VRH, Gardner 4LW*
Weight:	5½ tons	Transmission:	3-speed, chain
Wheel Diameter:	1 ft 6 in	Horsepower:	40 hp at 1,200 rpm
Gauge:	3 ft	Tractive Effort:	2,950 lbs

Fleet No	Makers No	Allocation	Remarks
☐ **LM 77 H***	329680	–	Preserved. See note (1)
☐ **LM 78 H**	329682	Clonsast	Formerly No 9
☐ **LM 79 H**	329683	Ballydermot	Formerly No 10. Scrapped
☐ **LM 80 H**	329688	Timahoe	Formerly No 13
☐ **LM 81 H***	329686	Clonsast	Out of use
☐ **LM 82***	329688	Timahoe	
☐ **LM 83**	329690	Ummeras	Formerly No 1
☐ **LM 84 J**	329691	Timahoe	Formerly No 14
☐ **LM 85 J***	329693	Mountdillon	
☐ **LM 86 J**	329695	Mountdillon	
☐ **LM 87 J**	329696	–	Preserved. See note (2)
☐ **LM 88 J**	329698	Ballydermot	Formerly No 16

☐	**LM 89 J***	329700	Coolnagun	Out of use
☐	**LM 90 J***	329701	Ballivor	
☐	**LM 91†**	371962	Boora	
☐	**LM 92 L†**	371967	–	Preserved. See note (3)

(1) Preserved at Cumann Traenach Gaeltacht Lair, Fintown Station, County Donegal
(2) Preserved at Irish Narrow Gauge Trust, Dromod Station, County Leitrim
(3) Preserved at Tralee & Dingle Steam Railway, Blennerville, County Kerry

RUSTON & HORNSBY 48DL   4wDM

Built:	1954	Engine:	Ruston 3VRH, Gardner 4LW*
Weight:	7 tons	Transmission:	3-speed, twin ratio, chain
Wheel Diameter:	1 ft 6 in	Horsepower:	48 hp at 1,200 rpm
Gauge:	3 ft	Tractive Effort:	3,780 lbs

Fleet No	Makers No	Allocation	Remarks
☐ **LM 93 T***	373376	Ballydermot	
☐ **LM 94 T**	373377	Ballydermot	
☐ **LM 95 T**	373379	Lullymore	Out of use

RUSTON & HORNSBY 40DL   4wDM

Built:	1954	Engine:	Ruston 3VRH
Weight:	5½ tons	Transmission:	3-speed, chain
Wheel Diameter:	1 ft 6 in	Horsepower:	40 hp at 1200rpm
Gauge:	3 ft	Tractive Effort:	2,950 lbs

Fleet No	Makers No	Allocation	Remarks
☐ **LM 96 L**	375314	Bangor Erris	

RUSTON & HORNSBY 48DL   4wDM

Built:	1954	Engine:	Ruston 4VRH, Gardner 4LW*
Weight:	7 tons	Transmission:	3-speed, twin ratio, chain
Wheel Diameter:	1 ft 6 in	Horsepower:	48 hp at 1,200 rpm
Gauge:	3 ft	Tractive Effort:	3,780 lbs

Fleet No	Makers No	Allocation	Remarks
☐ **LM 97 T**	375332	Lullymore	Out of use
☐ **LM 98 T**	375335	Clonsast	Out of use
☐ **LM 99 U**	375336	Bellair	
☐ **LM 100***	375341	Derrygreenagh	
☐ **LM 101 U**	379059	Boora	
☐ **LM 102**	379076	Bellair	
☐ **LM 103**	375318	Boora	
☐ **LM 104***	375322	Bangor Erris	Formerly No 8
☐ **LM 105 U**	375344	Blackwater	
☐ **LM 106 U**	375345	Mountdillon	
☐ **LM 107 U**	379055	Boora	
☐ **LM 108 U***	379061	Tionnsca	
☐ **LM 109 U***	397064	Boora	Out of use
☐ **LM 110 U**	397066	Boora	

RUSTON & HORNSBY 40DL 4wDM

Built:	1954
Weight:	5½ tons
Wheel Diameter:	1 ft 6 in
Gauge:	3 ft

Engine:	Ruston 3VRH
Transmission:	3-speed, chain
Horsepower:	40 hp at 1,200 rpm
Tractive Effort:	2,950 lbs

Fleet No	Makers No	Allocation	Remarks
☐ **LM 111**	379079	Blackwater	See note (1)

(1) Used on the Clonmacnoise & West Offaly Railway, painted in a yellow and green livery

RUSTON & HORNSBY LBT 4wDM

Built:	1954
Weight:	4½ tons
Wheel Diameter:	1 ft 4⅚ in
Gauge:	2 ft

Engine:	Ruston 3VSH
Transmission:	3-speed, chain
Horsepower:	31½ hp
Tractive Effort:	

Fleet No	Makers No	Allocation	Remarks
☐ **LM 112**	375699	Kilberry	Out of use

RUSTON & HORNSBY 48DL 4wDM

Built:	1954
Weight:	7 tons
Wheel Diameter:	1 ft 6 in
Gauge:	3 ft

Engine:	Ruston 4VRH, Gardner 4LW*
Transmission:	3-speed, twin ratio, chain
Horsepower:	48 hp at 1,200 rpm
Tractive Effort:	3,780 lbs

Fleet No	Makers No	Allocation	Remarks
☐ **LM 113 U***	379068	Derrygreenagh	
☐ **LM 114 U***	379070	Boora	
☐ **LM 115 U**	379073	Kilberry	

2ft gauge R&H
LBT LM112 in
action at Kilberry,
County Kildare,
in August 1973.
Peter Nicholson

RUSTON & HORNSBY 40DL

	4wDM		
Built:	1954	*Engine:*	Ruston 3VRH
Weight:	5½ tons	*Transmission:*	3-speed, chain
Wheel Diameter:	1 ft 6 in	*Horsepower:*	40 hp at 1,200 rpm
Gauge:	3 ft	*Tractive Effort:*	2, 950 lbs

Fleet No	Makers No	Allocation	Remarks
☐ **LM 116 M**	379077	Tionnsca	Formerly No 15

RUSTON & HORNSBY 48DL

	4wDM, 4wDH‡		
Built:	1954	*Engine:*	Ruston 4VRH, Gardner 4LW*
Weight:	7 tons	*Transmission:*	3-speed, twin ratio, chain
Wheel Diameter:	1 ft 6 in	*Horsepower:*	48 hp at 1,200 rpm
Gauge:	3 ft	*Tractive Effort:*	3,780 lbs

Fleet No	Makers No	Allocation	Remarks
☐ **LM 117 U**	379910	Boora	
☐ **LM 118 V**	379913	Boora	
☐ **LM 119 V**	379916	Tionnsca	Out of use
☐ **LM 120 V**	379917	Coolnamona	Dismantled
☐ **LM 121 V***	379922	Derrygreenagh	
☐ **LM 122 V**	379923	Boora	
☐ **LM 123***	379925	Tionnsca	Rebuilt with Clarke hydraulic transmission. Note (1)

(1) Used on the Bellacorick Bog Railway, in a grey and green livery, to take visitors on guided tours around the Oweninny system in Co Mayo, hauling the passenger saloon from a former West Clare section railcar.

RUSTON & HORNSBY 40DL

	4wDM		
Built:	1954, 1955†	*Engine:*	Ruston 3VRH, Gardner 4LW*
Weight:	5½ tons	*Transmission:*	3-speed, chain
Wheel Diameter:	1 ft 6 in	*Horsepower:*	40 hp at 1,200 rpm
Gauge:	3 ft	*Tractive Effort:*	2,950 lbs

Fleet No	Makers No	Allocation	Remarks
☐ **LM 124 N†**	379081	Clonsast	Out of use
☐ **LM 125 O***	379084	Derrygreenagh	

RUSTON & HORNSBY 48DL

	4wDM		
Built:	1954, 1955†	*Engine:*	Ruston 4VRH
Weight:	7 tons	*Transmission:*	3-speed, twin ratio, chain
Wheel Diameter:	1 ft 6 in	*Horsepower:*	48 hp at 1,200 rpm
Gauge:	3 ft	*Tractive Effort:*	3,780 lbs

Fleet No	Makers No	Allocation	Remarks
☐ **LM 126 W**	379927	Boora	
☐ **LM 127 W**	379928	Boora	
☐ **LM 128 X†**	383260	Blackwater	
☐ **LM 129 X**	383264	Mountdillon	

R&H 48DL LM128 at Blackwater, County Offaly, on 2nd August 1995.

RUSTON & HORNSBY 40DL

		4wDM
Built:	1955, 1956†	Engine:	Ruston 3VRH, Gardner 4LW*
Weight:	5½ tons	Transmission:	3-speed, chain
Wheel Diameter:	1 ft 6 in	Horsepower:	40 hp at 1,200 rpm
Gauge:	3 ft	Tractive Effort:	2,950 lbs

Fleet No	Makers No	Allocation	Remarks
☐ **LM 130 P**	382812	Kilberry	
☐ **LM 131**	379086	Boora	Out of use
☐ **LM 132 P**	382809	Derrygreenagh	
☐ **LM 133 P**	379090	Derrygreenagh	Out of use
☐ **LM 134 Q**	382811	Derrygreenagh	
☐ **LM 135 Q**	382814	Derrygreenagh	Incorrectly carries works plate No 382841
☐ **LM 136 Q**	382815	Derrygreenagh	Out of use
☐ **LM 137 Q**	382817	Tionnsca	Formerly No 6
☐ **LM 138 Q**	382819	Tionnsca	
☐ **LM 139 Q***	392137	Littleton	Out of use
☐ **LM 140 Q***	392139	Ballivor	
☐ **LM 141 Q**	392142	Boora	Out of use
☐ **LM 142 Q**	392145	Boora	Out of use
☐ **LM 143†***	392148	Blackwater	
☐ **LM 144 Q†**	392149	Derrygreenagh	

RUSTON & HORNSBY 48 DL

		4wDM
Built:	1956	Engine:	Ruston 4VRH, Gardner 4LW*
Weight:	7 tons	Transmission:	3-speed, twin ratio, chain
Wheel Diameter:	1 ft 6 in	Horsepower:	48 hp at 1,200 rpm
Gauge:	3 ft	Tractive Effort:	3,780 lbs

Fleet No	Makers No	Allocation	Remarks
☐ **LM 145 X**	394023	Derrygreenagh	
☐ **LM 146***	394024	Ballydermot	Out of use
☐ **LM 147 X**	394025	Ballydermot	Out of use
☐ **LM 148 X**	394026	Derrygreenagh	
☐ **LM 149 X***	394028	Derrygreenagh	
☐ **LM 150 X***	394027	Derrygreenagh	

RUSTON & HORNSBY 40DL

Built:	1956	*Engine:*	Ruston 3VRH, Gardner 4LW*
Weight:	5½ tons	*Transmission:*	3-speed, chain
Wheel Diameter:	1 ft 6 in	*Horsepower:*	40 hp at 1,200 rpm
Gauge:	3 ft	*Tractive Effort:*	2,950 lbs

4wDM

Fleet No	Makers No	Allocation	Remarks
☐ **LM 151 Q***	392150	Blackwater	
☐ **LM 152 Q***	392151	Ballivor	

RUSTON & HORNSBY 48DL

Built:	1956	*Engine:*	Ruston 4VRH, Gardner 4LW*
Weight:	7 tons	*Transmission:*	3-speed, twin ratio, chain
Wheel Diameter:	1 ft 6 in	*Horsepower:*	48 hp at 1,200 rpm
Gauge:	3 ft	*Tractive Effort:*	3,780 lbs

4wDM

Fleet No	Makers No	Allocation	Remarks
☐ **LM 153 Q**	394031	Mountdillon	
☐ **LM 154 X**	394030	Blackwater	
☐ **LM 155 X***	394031	Mountdillon	
☐ **LM 156 X**	394032	Derrygreenagh	
☐ **LM 157 X***	394033	Derrygreenagh	
☐ **LM 158 X***	394034	Derrygreenagh	
☐ **LM 159 X**	402174	Derrygreenagh	
☐ **LM 160 X**	402176	Ballivor	
☐ **LM 161 X**	402175	Boora	
☐ **LM 162 X**	402177	Tionnsca	
☐ **LM 163 X***	402178	Boora	

RUSTON & HORNSBY 40DL

Built:	1956	*Engine:*	Ruston 3VRH, Gardner 4LW*
Weight:	5½ tons	*Transmission:*	3-speed, chain
Wheel Diameter:	1 ft 6 in	*Horsepower:*	40 hp at 1,200 rpm
Gauge:	3 ft	*Tractive Effort:*	2,950 lbs

4wDM

Fleet No	Makers No	Allocation	Remarks
☐ **LM 164 Q***	392152	Clonkeen	

RUSTON & HORNSBY 48DL — 4wDM

Built:	1956
Weight:	7 tons
Wheel Diameter:	1 ft 6 in
Gauge:	3 ft

Engine:	Ruston 4VRH, Gardner 4LW*
Transmission:	3-speed, twin ratio, chain
Horsepower:	48 hp at 1,200 rpm
Tractive Effort:	3,780 lbs

Fleet No	Makers No	Allocation	Remarks
☐ LM 165*	402179	Derrygreenagh	

RUSTON & HORNSBY 40DL — 4wDM

Built:	1956
Weight:	5½ tons
Wheel Diameter:	1 ft 6 in
Gauge:	3 ft

Engine:	Ruston 3VRH, Gardner 4LW*
Transmission:	3-speed, chain
Horsepower:	40 hp at 1,200 rpm
Tractive Effort:	2,950 lbs

Fleet No	Makers No	Allocation	Remarks
☐ LM 166 Q*	402977	Ballivor	
☐ LM 167 Q*	402928	Coolnamona	
☐ LM 168 Q	402980	Derrygreenagh	
☐ LM 169 Q	402981	Derrygreenagh	
☐ LM 170 Q*	402982	Templetouhy	
☐ LM 171 Q	402983	Boora	Out of use
☐ LM 172 Q	402984	Coolnagun	Out of use
☐ LM 173 Q*	402985	Lemanaghan	
☐ LM 174 Q	402986	Tionnsca	

RUSTON & HORNSBY PROTOTYPE — 0-4-0DH

Built:	1958
Weight:	8 tons
Wheel Diameter:	
Gauge:	3 ft

Engine:	Ruston 6YC. Later fitted with a Ford engine
Transmission:	Hydraulic
Horsepower:	75 hp
Tractive Effort:	

Fleet No	Makers No	Allocation	Remarks
☐ LM 175	420042	Boora	Now has mechanical transmission.

Special Ruston & Hornsby prototype built for Bord na Móna which led to a second prototype, LM 176, built by the Bord

BORD NA MÓNA WAGONMASTER — 0-4-0DM

Built:	1961
Weight:	8 tons
Wheel Diameter:	
Gauge:	3 ft

Engine:	Ford 849P
Transmission:	
Horsepower:	80 hp
Tractive Effort:	

Fleet No	Makers No	Allocation	Remarks
☐ LM 176	–	Derrygreenagh	See below

Home built prototype following on from LM 175, which utimately led to the Hunslet Wagonmasters

Above:
Special R&H prototype LM175, built for Bord na Móna, seen at Ferbane Power Station on 3rd August 1995.

Right:
Home-built Wagonmaster prototype LM176, forerunner of the Hunslet Wagon-masters.
Midland Publishing Limited collection.

RUSTON & HORNSBY 33/40HP

4wDM

Built:	1943	Engine:	Ruston 3VRO, Gardner 4LW*
Weight:	5 tons	Transmission:	3-speed, chain
Wheel Diameter:	1 ft 6 in	Horsepower:	40 hp at 1,200 rpm
Gauge:	3 ft	Tractive Effort:	2,950 lbs

Fleet No	Makers No	Allocation	Remarks
☐ **LM 177***	218037	Littleton	Ex S & L Minerals No 5, Wirksworth, acquired 1960.

DEUTZ KS28B

		0-4-0DM	
Built:	1960	Engine:	Deutz A2L514 2 cylinder
Weight:	3.4 tons	Transmission:	4-speed mechanical
Wheel Diameter:	1 ft 4⅜ in	Horsepower:	28 hp
Gauge:	3 ft	Tractive Effort:	

Fleet No	Makers No	Allocation	Remarks
☐ **LM 178**	57120	Boora	Out of use
☐ **LM 179**	57121	Boora	Out of use
☐ **LM 180**	57122	Boora	Out of use
☐ **LM 181**	57123	Boora	Out of use
☐ **LM 182**	57126	Tionnsca	Dismantled
☐ **LM 183**	57127	Boora	Out of use
☐ **LM 184**	57130	Blackwater	
☐ **LM 185**	57131	Boora	
☐ **LM 186**	57132	Boora	Out of use
☐ **LM 187**	57133	Boora	Out of use
☐ **LM 188**	57124	Blackwater	
☐ **LM 189**	57129	Derrygreenagh	Formerly No 2. Out of use
☐ **LM 190**	57128	Derrygreenagh	Out of use
☐ **LM 191**	57134	Derrygreenagh	Formerly No 4. Out of use
☐ **LM 192**	57125	Derrygreenagh	Out of use
☐ **LM 193**	57135	Derrygreenagh	
☐ **LM 194**	57136	Blackwater	Formerly No 7.
☐ **LM 195**	57137	Tionnsca	Dismantled
☐ **LM 196**	57138	Tionnsca	Out of use
☐ **LM 197**	57139	Derrygreenagh	

*Deutz KS28B
LM181, at Boora,
County Offaly, on
3rd August 1995.*

*2ft gauge
Ruston & Hornsby
48DLU LM198
at Bellacorick,
County Mayo,
1st August 1995.*

RUSTON & HORNSBY 48DLU

		4wDM	
Built:	1956	Engine:	Ruston 4YC, Gardner 4LW*
Weight:	7 tons	Transmission:	3-speed, twin ratio, chain
Wheel Diameter:	1 ft 6 in	Horsepower:	48 hp at 1,200 rpm
Gauge:	2 ft	Tractive Effort:	3,780 lbs

Fleet No	Makers No	Allocation	Remarks
☐ **LM 198***	398076	Glenties	Acquired 1962, ex- ?. Delivered new to Charles Brand, Contractors, 9th July 1954.

HUNSLET WAGONMASTER

		0-4-0DM, 4wDH ‡	
Built:	1962, 1963†	Engine:	Ford 590E 6 cylinder, Cummins 6B 5.9L 6-cylinder ‡
Weight:	9.3 tons	Transmission:	4-speed with fluid coupling, Clarke hydraulic ‡
Wheel Diameter:	1ft 9in, 2ft 4in ‡	Horsepower:	85 bhp at 2,000 rpm, 115 bhp ‡
Gauge:	3 ft	Tractive Effort:	12,000 lbs

Fleet No	Makers No	Allocation	Remarks
☐ **LM 199 ‡**	6232	Derrygreenagh	Rebuilt in 1994. See note (1)
☐ **LM 200**	6233	Boora	
☐ **LM 201**	6234	Tionnsca	
☐ **LM 202 †**	6235	Tionnsca	
☐ **LM 203**	6236	Boora	
☐ **LM 204 † ‡**	6237	Derrygreenagh	Rebuilt in 1993. See note (1)
☐ **LM 205 †**	6238	Tionnsca	
☐ **LM 206 †**	6239	Boora	
☐ **LM 207 †**	6240	Bangor Erris	
☐ **LM 208 †**	6241	Derrygreenagh	
☐ **LM 209 †**	6242	Tionnsca	
☐ **LM 210 † ‡**	6243	Derrygreenagh	Rebuilt in 1992. See note (1)
☐ **LM 211 †**	6244	Derrygreenagh	
☐ **LM 212 †**	6245	Bangor Erris	
☐ **LM 213 †**	6246	Derrygreenagh	

Hunslet Wagonmaster LM202 at Tionnsca Abhainn Einne (Oweninny), County Mayo, on 18th July 1973. Peter Nicholson

☐	**LM 214** †	6247	Tionnsca	
☐	**LM 215** †	6248	Derrygreenagh	
☐	**LM 216** †	6249	Boora	
☐	**LM 217** †	6250	Bangor Erris	
☐	**LM 218** † ‡	6251	Derrygreenagh	Rebuilt in 1994. See note (1)
☐	**LM 219** †	6252	Boora	
☐	**LM 220** †	6253	Boora	
☐	**LM 221** †	6254	Derrygreenagh	
☐	**LM 222** †	6255	Blackwater	
☐	**LM 223** † ‡	6256	Derrygreenagh	Rebuilt in 1993. See note (1)

(1) Rebuilt by Bord na Móna at Derrygreenagh Works as a diesel-hydraulic.

RUSTON & HORNSBY 40DL   4wDM

Built:	1954	Engine:	Ruston 3VRH
Weight:	5½ tons	Transmission:	3-speed, chain
Wheel Diameter:	1 ft 6 in	Horsepower:	40 hp at 1,200 rpm
Gauge:	2 ft	Tractive Effort:	2,950 lbs

	Fleet No	Makers No	Allocation	Remarks
☐	**LM 224**	375317	Kilberry	Acquired c1963, ex -?-. Delivered new to Cementation Co Ltd, 24th August 1954.

R&H 40DL
LM224 at Kilberry,
County Kildare, on
10th July 1973.
Peter Nicholson

HUNSLET WAGONMASTER

0-4-0DM, 4wDH ‡

Built:	1964, 1965 †	Engine:	Ford 590E 6 cylinder, Cummins 6B 5.9L 6-cylinder ‡
Weight:	9.3 tons	Transmission:	4-speed with fluid coupling, Clarke hydraulic ‡
Wheel Diameter:	1ft 9in, 2ft 4in ‡	Horsepower:	85 bhp at 2,000 rpm, 115 bhp ‡
Gauge:	3 ft	Tractive Effort:	12,000 lbs

Fleet No	Makers No	Allocation	Remarks
☐ **LM 225** ‡	6304	Derrygreenagh	Rebuilt by Bord na Móna in 1994. See note (1)
☐ **LM 226** ‡	6305	Mountdillon	Rebuilt by Bord na Móna in 1994. See note (2)
☐ **LM 227**	6306	Boora	
☐ **LM 228**	6307	Boora	
☐ **LM 229**	6308	Blackwater	Renumbered LM 294
☐ **LM 230**	6309	Blackwater	
☐ **LM 231**	6310	Blackwater	
☐ **LM 232**	6311	Derrygreenagh	
☐ **LM 233** †	6312	Boora	
☐ **LM 234** †	6313	Blackwater	
☐ **LM 235** †	6314	Boora	
☐ **LM 236** †	6315	Lullymore	
☐ **LM 237** †	6316	Bellair	
☐ **LM 238** †	6318	Derrygreenagh	
☐ **LM 239** †	6317	Derrygreenagh	
☐ **LM 240** †	6319	Boora	
☐ **LM 241** †	6320	Ballydermot	
☐ **LM 242** †	6321	Mountdillon	
☐ **LM 243** †	6322	Boora	
☐ **LM 244** †	6323	Boora	
☐ **LM 245** †	6324	Boora	
☐ **LM 246** †	6325	Boora	
☐ **LM 247** †	6326	Mountdillon	Out of use
☐ **LM 248** †	6328	Mountdillon	
☐ **LM 249** †	6327	Mountdillon	
☐ **LM 250** †	6329	Mountdillon	
☐ **LM 251** †	6330	Tionnsca	
☐ **LM 252** †	6331	Mountdillon	

(1) Rebuilt at Derrygreenagh Works as a diesel-hydraulic.
(2) Rebuilt at Mountdillon Works as a diesel-hydraulic.

The distinctive cast plate carried by the Hunslet-built Wagonmasters on the bonnet side.
Peter Nicholson

DEUTZ KS28B

		0-4-0DM	
Built:	1965	Engine:	Deutz A2L514 2-cylinder
Weight:	3.4 tons	Transmission:	4-speed mechanical
Wheel Diameter:	1 ft 4⅜ in	Horsepower:	28 hp
Gauge:	3 ft	Tractive Effort:	

Fleet No	Makers No	Allocation	Remarks
☐ **LM 253**	57834	Blackwater	
☐ **LM 254**	57835	Blackwater	
☐ **LM 255**	57838	Coolnamona	Out of use
☐ **LM 256**	57837	Boora	
☐ **LM 257**	57836	Derrygreenagh	
☐ **LM 258**	57839	Mountdillon	
☐ **LM 259**	57840	Boora	
☐ **LM 260**	57841	Boora	Out of use
☐ **LM 261**	57842	Blackwater	
☐ **LM 262**	57843	Mountdillon	Out of use

RUSTON & HORNSBY LBT

		4wDM	
Built:	1968	Engine:	Ruston 2YDA
Weight:	3¾ tons	Transmission:	3-speed, chain
Wheel Diameter:	1 ft 4⁵⁄₆ in	Horsepower:	31½ hp at 1,200 rpm
Gauge:	2 ft	Tractive Effort:	

Fleet No	Makers No	Allocation	Remarks
☐ **LM 263**	7002/0600-1	Glenties	

2ft gauge
R&H LAT LM264
at Kilberry,
County Kildare,
10th July 1973.
Peter Nicholson

RUSTON & HORNSBY LAT

		4wDM	
Built:	1954	Engine:	Ruston 2VSH
Weight:	3½ tons	Transmission:	3-speed, chain
Wheel Diameter:	1 ft 4⅚ in	Horsepower:	20 hp at 1,200 rpm
Gauge:	2 ft	Tractive Effort:	

Fleet No	Makers No	Allocation	Remarks
☐ LM 264	371535	Glenties	Acquired c1970, ex- -?-. Delivered new to Ruddock & Meighan 6th December 1954.

RUSTON & HORNSBY LBT

		4wDM	
Built:	1954	Engine:	Ruston 3VSH
Weight:	3¾ tons	Transmission:	3-speed, chain
Wheel Diameter:	1 ft 4⅚ in	Horsepower:	31½ hp at 1,200 rpm
Gauge:	3 ft	Tractive Effort:	

Fleet No	Makers No	Allocation	Remarks
☐ LM 265	375696	Kilberry	Ex-Pelton Brick Co (delivered 12th July 1954) via ME Engineering, London, c1970.

HUNSLET WAGONMASTER

		0-4-0DM	
Built:	1971, 1972†	Engine:	Ford 2713E 6-cylinder
Weight:	9.3 tons	Transmission:	5-speed with fluid coupling
Wheel Diameter:	1 ft 9 in	Horsepower:	85 bhp at 2,000 rpm
Gauge:	3 ft	Tractive Effort:	12,000 lbs

Fleet No	Makers No	Allocation	Remarks
☐ LM 266	7232	Boora	
☐ LM 267	7233	Mountdillon	
☐ LM 268	7234	Littleton	
☐ LM 269	7235	Boora	
☐ LM 270	7237	Mountdillon	
☐ LM 271	7236	Timahoe	
☐ LM 272	7239	Tionnsca	
☐ LM 273†	7246	Boora	
☐ LM 274	7238	Mountdillon	
☐ LM 275†	7240	Coolnamona	
☐ LM 276†	7241	Littleton	
☐ LM 277†	7242	Timahoe	
☐ LM 278†	7243	Blackwater	
☐ LM 279†	7244	Ballydermot	
☐ LM 280†	7245	Blackwater	
☐ LM 281†	7247	Blackwater	
☐ LM 282†	7248	Blackwater	
☐ LM 283†	7250	Derrygreenagh	
☐ LM 284†	7249	Ballydermot	
☐ LM 285†	7253	Ballydermot	
☐ LM 286†	7254	Blackwater	
☐ LM 287†	7255	Blackwater	
☐ LM 288†	7256	Blackwater	
☐ LM 289†	7252	Derrygreenagh	
☐ LM 290†	7251	Derrygreenagh	

*Hunslet
Wagonmaster
LM283
at Timahoe,
County Kildare,
19th July 1973.
Peter Nicholson*

RUSTON & HORNSBY LAT

		4wDM	
Built:	1958	Engine:	Ruston 2VSH
Weight:	3½ tons	Transmission:	3-speed, chain
Wheel Diameter:	1 ft 4⁵⁄₆ in	Horsepower:	20 hp at 1,200 rpm
Gauge:	3 ft	Tractive Effort:	

Fleet No	Makers No	Allocation	Remarks
☐ **LM 291**	421428	Timahoe	Ex-Johnson's Rolls Limited and A Cocklin, Bucks. Imported August 1973. Out of use

HUNSLET WAGONMASTER

		0-4-0DM, 4wDH ‡	
Built:	1977, 79†, 80*	Engine:	Ford 2713E 6 cylinder, Cummins 6B 5.9L 6-cylinder ‡
Weight:	9.3 tons	Transmission:	5-speed with fluid coupling,Clarke hydraulic.‡
Wheel Diameter:	1ft 9in, 2ft 4in ‡	Horsepower:	85 bhp at 2,000 rpm, 115 bhp ‡
Gauge:	3 ft	Tractive Effort:	12,000 lbs

Fleet No	Makers No	Allocation	Remarks
☐ **LM 292**	8529	Blackwater	
☐ **LM 293**	8530	Blackwater	
☐ **LM 294**	8531	Blackwater	
☐ **LM 295** ‡	8532	Blackwater	Rebuilt in 1993. See note (1)
☐ **LM 296**	8534	Blackwater	
☐ **LM 297**	8533	Boora	
☐ **LM 298**	8538	Boora	
☐ **LM 299**	8537	Derrygreenagh	
☐ **LM 300**	8535	Mountdillon	
☐ **LM 301**	8536	Ballydermot	
☐ **LM 302**	8539	Mountdillon	
☐ **LM 303**	8540	Derrygreenagh	
☐ **LM 304**	8543	Bangor Erris	

☐	**LM 305**	8544	Derrygreenagh	
☐	**LM 306**	8541	Boora	
☐	**LM 307**	8542	Boora	
☐	**LM 308**	8546	Derrygreenagh	
☐	**LM 309**	8545	Templetouhy	
☐	**LM 310**	8547	Derrygreenagh	
☐	**LM 311** *	8551	Littleton	Built 1980
☐	**LM 311**	8930	Blackwater	Formerly numbered LM 332
☐	**LM 312**	8550	Blackwater	
☐	**LM 313**	8549	Blackwater	
☐	**LM 314**	8548	Templetouhy	
☐	**LM 315** †	8922	Blackwater	

(1) Rebuilt by Bord na Móna at Blackwater Works as a diesel-hydraulic. ‡

SIMPLEX 60SL

Built:	1980	4wDM	
Weight:	5 tons	Engine:	Lister HR4 air cooled
Wheel Diameter:	1 ft 6 in	Transmission:	3-speed, chain
Gauge:	3 ft	Horsepower:	50 hp at 1,800 rpm
		Tractive Effort:	

Fleet No	Makers No	Allocation	Remarks
☐ **LM 316**	60SL741	Kilberry	
☐ **LM 317**	60SL742	Kilberry	

HUNSLET WAGONMASTER

Built:	1977, 1979 †,	0-4-0DM	
	1980 ‡, 1981 *	Engine:	Ford 2713E 6 cylinder
Weight:	9.3 tons	Transmission:	5-speed with fluid coupling
Wheel Diameter:	1 ft 9 in	Horsepower:	85 bhp at 2,000 rpm
Gauge:	3 ft	Tractive Effort:	12,000 lbs

Fleet No	Makers No	Allocation	Remarks
☐ **LM 318** †	8925	Mountdillon	
☐ **LM 319** †	8926	Boora	
☐ **LM 320** ‡	8939	Blackwater	
☐ **LM 321** ‡	8927	Littleton	
☐ **LM 322** †	8923	Blackwater	
☐ **LM 323** †	8924	Blackwater	See note (1)
☐ **LM 324** ‡	8931	Derrygreenagh	
☐ **LM 325** *	8942	Littleton	
☐ **LM 326** ‡	8932	Blackwater	
☐ **LM 327** ‡	8933	Coolnamona	
☐ **LM 328** ‡	8935	Littleton	
☐ **LM 329** ‡	8936	Littleton	
☐ **LM 330** ‡	8937	Mountdillon	
☐ **LM 331** ‡	8934	Blackwater	
☐ **LM 332**	8551	Littleton	Now numbered LM 311
☐ **LM 333** *	8940	Templetouhy	
☐ **LM 334** *	8941	Blackwater	

	LM 335 ‡	8938	Littleton
	LM 336 *	8943	Blackwater
	LM 337 *	8944	Ballydermot
	LM 338 *	8945	Littleton
	LM 339 *	8946	Derrygreenagh
	LM 340 *	8928	Blackwater

(1) LM322 and LM323 are used on the Clonmacnoise & West Offaly Railway. They are painted in a yellow and green livery.

SIMPLEX 60SL

4wDM

Built:	1980	Engine:	Lister HR4 air cooled
Weight:	5 tons	Transmission:	3-speed, chain
Wheel Diameter:	1 ft 6 in	Horsepower:	50 hp at 1,800 rpm
Gauge:	3 ft	Tractive Effort:	

Fleet No	Makers No	Allocation	Remarks
☐ LM 341	60SL740	Coolnagun	Out of use

HUNSLET WAGONMASTER

0-4-0DM

Built:	1980	Engine:	Ford 2713E 6 cylinder
Weight:	9.3 tons	Transmission:	5-speed with fluid coupling
Wheel Diameter:	1 ft 9 in	Horsepower:	85 bhp at 2,000 rpm
Gauge:	3 ft	Tractive Effort:	12,000 lbs

Fleet No	Makers No	Allocation	Remarks
☐ LM 342	8929	Blackwater	

SIMPLEX 60SL

4wDM

Built:	1980	Engine:	Lister HR4 air cooled
Weight:	5 tons	Transmission:	3-speed, chain
Wheel Diameter:	1 ft 6 in	Horsepower:	50 hp at 1,800 rpm
Gauge:	3 ft	Tractive Effort:	

Fleet No	Makers No	Allocation	Remarks
☐ LM 343	60SL746	Blackwater	
☐ LM 344	60SL751	Mountdillon	
☐ LM 345	60SL749	Tionnsca	Dismantled
☐ LM 346	60SL747	Attymon	
☐ LM 347	60SL750	–	Dismantled. See note (1)
☐ LM 348	60SL744	Boora	
☐ LM 349	60SL743	Kilberry	
☐ LM 350	60SL748	–	See note (2)
☐ LM 351	60SL745	Kilberry	Out of use

(1) LM347 is owned by the Cavan & Leitrim Railway, stored as a spares source at a private location.
(2) LM350 is owned by the Cavan & Leitrim Railway, Dromod, in working order.

Simplex 60SL LM348 at Boora, County Offaly, on 3rd August 1995.

HIBBERD	4wDM		
Built:	1962	Engine:	
Weight:		Transmission:	
Wheel Diameter:		Horsepower:	
Gauge:	2 ft	Tractive Effort:	

Fleet No	Makers No	Allocation	Remarks
☐ **LM 352**	3989	Kilberry	Ex-CSET (Irish Sugar, Gowla Farm, No 5). Acquired 1983. Scrapped

Gleismac LF45 LM366 at Blackwater, County Offaly, on 2nd August 1995.

RUSTON & HORNSBY LBT — 4wDM

Built:	1963	Engine:	Ruston 2YDA
Weight:	3 tons	Transmission:	3-speed, chain
Wheel Diameter:	1ft 4⁵⁄₁₆ in	Horsepower:	31½ hp at 1,200 rpm
Gauge:	2 ft	Tractive Effort:	

Fleet No	Makers No	Allocation	Remarks
☐ **LM 353**	497771	Kilberry	Ex-CSET (Irish Sugar, Gowla Farm, No 6). Acquired 1983.

GLEISMAC LF45/DUNDALK ENGINEERING — 4wDH

Built:	1984	Engine:	Deutz F3L 912
Weight:	6 tons	Transmission:	Hydraulic, sauer torque converter
Wheel Diameter:		Horsepower:	49 hp
Gauge:	3 ft	Tractive Effort:	

Fleet No	Makers No	Allocation	Remarks
☐ **LM 354**		Blackwater	
☐ **LM 355**		Mountdillon	
☐ **LM 356**		Littleton	
☐ **LM 357**	None	Blackwater	
☐ **LM 358**		Ballivor	
☐ **LM 359**		Mountdillon	
☐ **LM 360**		Ballivor	
☐ **LM 361**	LM 361	Tionnsca	
☐ **LM 362**	LM 362	Bangor Erris	
☐ **LM 363**	LM 365	Boora	
☐ **LM 364**		Blackwater	
☐ **LM 365**	LM 365	Derryfadda	
☐ **LM 366**	None	Blackwater	
☐ **LM 367**	LM 367	Blackwater	
☐ **LM 368**	LM 368	Blackwater	
☐ **LM 369**		Boora	
☐ **LM 370**		Blackwater	
☐ **LM 371**		Blackwater	
☐ **LM 372**		Blackwater	
☐ **LM 373**		Blackwater	

Built by Dundalk Engineering Limited, Dundalk, County Louth, under licence from Gleismac Italiana SPA

GLEISMAC LF80 / DUNDALK ENGINEERING — 4wDH

Built:	1983	Engine:	Deutz
Weight:		Transmission:	Hydraulic
Wheel Diameter:		Horsepower:	80 hp
Gauge:	3 ft	Tractive Effort:	

Fleet No	Makers No	Allocation	Remarks
☐ **LM 374**	?	–	Fate unknown. See following note (1)
☐ **LM 375**	?	–	Fate unknown. See following note (1)

(1) The two latter-mentioned machines were demonstration locomotives built by Dundalk Engineering Ltd, County Louth, under licence from Gleismac Italiana SPA. They were delivered to Blackwater and later transferred to Mountdillon. An order was subsequently placed for 20 type LF45 locomotives, numbered LM354-LM373. The fate of the demonstrators is unknown, but the numbers LM374-LM375 were re-used on the first two Hunslet diesel-hydraulic locomotives in the LM374-LM388 batch, immediately below.

HUNSLET

HUNSLET		4wDH		
Built:	1984, 1985 †, 1986 ‡		*Engine:*	Ford 2725, 6-cylinder
Weight:	9 tons	*Transmission:*	Hydraulic, Clarke 28000 series torque converter	
Wheel Diameter:	2 ft 4 in	*Horsepower:*	115 hp	
Gauge:	3 ft	*Tractive Effort:*		

Fleet No	Makers No	Allocation	Remarks
☐ **LM 374**	9239	Mountdillon	
☐ **LM 375**	9240	Mountdillon	
☐ **LM 376**	9241	Mountdillon	
☐ **LM 377**	9243	Mountdillon	
☐ **LM 378**	9242	Blackwater	
☐ **LM 379 †**	9251	Littleton	
☐ **LM 380 †**	9252	Coolnamona	
☐ **LM 381 †**	9253	Blackwater	
☐ **LM 382 ‡**	9254	Derrygreenagh	
☐ **LM 383 ‡**	9255	Derrygreenagh	
☐ **LM 384 ‡**	9256	Boora	
☐ **LM 385 ‡**	9257	Mountdillon	
☐ **LM 386 ‡**	9258	Blackwater	
☐ **LM 387 ‡**	9259	Boora	
☐ **LM 388 ‡**	9272	Littleton	

LM375, one of the pair of elusive Gleismac LF80 demonstrators, rests on the Mountdillon system, 9th September 1983.
Dave Holroyd

BORD NA MÓNA

4wDH

Built:	1994, 1995 † 1996 ‡	Engine:	Cummins 6B 5.9L 6-cylinder, Iveco 8061.25 6-cylinder ‡
Weight:	9½ tons	Transmission:	Hydraulic, Clarke-Hurth type 12.5LHR28365-1
Wheel Diameter:	2 ft 4in	Horsepower:	115 hp, 170 hp at 2,700 rpm ‡
Gauge:	3 ft	Tractive Effort:	

Fleet No	Makers No	Allocation	Remarks
☐ **LM 389**		Blackwater	
☐ **LM 390**		Blackwater	
☐ **LM 391**		Boora	
☐ **LM 392** †		Boora	
☐ **LM 393** †		Boora	
☐ **LM 394** ‡		Boora	
☐ **LM 395** †		Blackwater	
☐ **LM 396** †		Blackwater	
☐ **LM 397**			Note (1)
☐ **LM 398**			Note (1)
☐ **LM 399**			Note (1)
☐ **LM 400**			Note (1)
☐ **LM 401**			Note (1)

(1) It is anticipated that a further batch of these locomotives will be built by Bord na Mona in 1996 and will carry these numbers when completed.

Bord na Móna 4wDH LM391 brings a rake of empty wagons through Kylemore Lock on the disused Ballinasloe branch of the Grand Canal, part of which has been converted to a Bord na Móna railway, on 2nd August 1995.

Hunslet 4wDH LM377 (left) and 0-4-0DM Wagonmaster LM249 at Blackwater, County Offaly, on 2nd August 1995.

An unidentified Wagonmaster brings a loaded rake of wagons into the reception sidings at Bellacorrick Power Station in County Mayo, on 1st August 1995.

RAILCARS

BORD NA MÓNA RAILCAR 4wPMR

Built:	?	Engine:	Ford E93A, 4 cylinder petrol
Weight:		Transmission:	Hydraulic
Wheel Diameter:		Horsepower:	
Gauge:	3 ft	Seating:	

Fleet No	Makers No	Allocation	Remarks
☐ **C11**	BnM	Clonsast	Formerly Railcar No 1. Sold or scrapped.
☐ **C12**	BnM	Clonsast	Formerly Railcar No 2. See note (1)

(1) Dismantled and in store at the Irish Narrow Gauge Trust, Dromod Station, County Leitrim
Both railcars were built at Clonsast.

WICKHAM TYPE 8BB RAILCAR 4wPMR

Built:	1938	Engine:	JAP 350cc petrol
Weight:		Transmission:	Mechanical
Wheel Diameter:		Horsepower:	
Gauge:	3 ft	Seating:	

Fleet No	Makers No	Allocation	Remarks
☐ **C13**	2449	–	Dismantled. Now at the Narrow Gauge Railway Centre, Gloddfa Ganol Slate Mine, Blaenau Ffestiniog

Bord na Móna 4wPMR railcar C11, parked at Clonsast, County Offaly, on 8th May 1986. Hamish Stevenson

WICKHAM TYPE 8S RAILCAR 2w+2wPMR

Built:	1948	Engine:	JAP 350cc, BSA petrol *. See note (5)
Weight:		Transmission:	Mechanical
Wheel Diameter:		Horsepower:	
Gauge:	3 ft, 2ft †	Seating:	

Fleet No	Makers No	Allocation	Remarks
☐ C14	4804	Ballydermot	Sold or scrapped
☐ C15	4805	Littleton	Sold or scrapped
☐ C16 * †	4806	Glenties	Dismantled
☐ C17 *	4807	Barna	Sold or scrapped
☐ C18 *	4808	–	See note (1)
☐ C19 *	4809	Littleton	Sold or scrapped
☐ C20 *	4810	–	Preserved. See note (2)
☐ C21	4811	Ballydermot	Sold or scrapped
☐ C22	4812	Ballydermot	Sold or scrapped
☐ C23	4813	–	Dismantled. See note (3)
☐ C24	4814	Ballydermot	Sold or scrapped
☐ C25	4815	Boora	Sold or scrapped
☐ C26	4816	–	See note (4)
☐ C27	4817	Clonsast	Sold or scrapped
☐ C28 *	4818	Lullymore	Scrapped
☐ C29 *	4819	Mountdillon	Sold or scrapped
☐ C30 *	4820	Mountdillon	Sold or scrapped

(1) Now at the Narrow Gauge Railway Centre, Gloddfa Ganol Slate Mine, Blaenau Ffestiniog
(2) Preserved by P D Nicholson at Radstock, Avon / N Somerset, c/o Somerset & Avon Railway
(3) Owned by P D Nicholson at Radstock, Avon / N Somerset, c/o Somerset & Avon Railwayt
(4) Now at the Narrow Gauge Railway Centre, Gloddfa Ganol Slate Mine, Blaenau Ffestiniog
(5) JAP engine replaced with BSA engine by Bord na Móna

Wickham type
14ST railcar C32
at Ballivor,
County Westmeath,
on 19th July 1973.
Peter Nicholson

WICKHAM TYPE 14ST RAILCAR

2w+2wPMR

Built:	1949	Engine:	Ford Petrol
Weight:		Transmission:	Mechanical
Wheel Diameter:		Horsepower:	
Gauge:	3 ft	Seating:	14

Fleet No	Makers No	Allocation	Remarks
☐ **C31**	4823	Mountdillon	Sold or scrapped. See note (1).
☐ **C32**	4824	Blackwater	Sold or scrapped. See note (1).

(1) C31 and C32 were supplied as part of a batch of three railcar trailers. Nos 4823 and 4824 were rebuilt by BnM as powered trolleys, but 4825 (see end of this section) remained an unpowered trailer.

Wickham type 17A railcar C34 at Timahoe, County Kildare, in July 1973.
Peter Nicholson

Bord na Móna / Southern Motors 4wPMR railcar C36, parked at Cloghan, County Offaly, on 10th August 1977.
Hamish Stevenson

WICKHAM TYPE 17A RAILCAR 2w+2wPMR

Built:	1949	Engine:	JAP 1323cc petrol
Weight:		Transmission:	Mechanical
Wheel Diameter:		Horsepower:	
Gauge:	3 ft	Seating:	

Fleet No	Makers No	Allocation	Remarks
☐ **C33**	4821	Clonsast	Sold or scrapped
☐ **C34**	4822	Timahoe	Sold or scrapped

BORD NA MÓNA/SOUTHERN MOTORS RAILCAR 4wPMR

Built:		Engine:	Ford Petrol
Weight:		Transmission:	Mechanical
Wheel Diameter:		Horsepower:	
Gauge:	3 ft	Seating:	

Fleet No	Makers No	Allocation	Remarks
☐ **C35**	1	Timahoe	Scrapped
☐ **C36**	2	Boora	Formerly numbered 36. Out of use

LOCOSPOOR TYPE EP RAILCAR 4wPMR

Built:		Engine:	Villiers Petrol
Weight:		Transmission:	Mechanical
Wheel Diameter:		Horsepower:	
Gauge:	3 ft	Seating:	

Fleet No	Makers No	Remarks
☐ **C37**	B7821E	Now at the Narrow Gauge Railway Centre, Gloddfa Ganol Slate Mine, Blaenau Ffestiniog

BORD NA MÓNA RAILCAR 4wPMR

Built:		Engine:	MWM Petrol
Weight:		Transmission:	Mechanical
Wheel Diameter:		Horsepower:	
Gauge:	3 ft	Seating:	

Fleet No	Makers No	Allocation	Remarks
☐ **C38**	BnM	Ballydermot	Formerly No 1. See note (1). Sold or scrapped

(1) Built by Bord na Móna at Ballydermot Works

WICKHAM TYPE 4S/BB RAILCAR

2w+2wPMR

Built:	1955	Engine:	JAP 600cc petrol
Weight:		Transmission:	
Wheel Diameter:		Horsepower:	
Gauge:	3 ft	Seating:	

	Fleet No	Makers No	Allocation	Remarks
☐	**C39**	6861	–	See note (1)
☐	**C40**	7127	Boora	Sold or scrapped
☐	**C41**	7128	Mountdillon	Sold or scrapped
☐	**C42**	7129	–	See note (2)
☐	**C43**	7130	Blackwater	
☐	**C44**	7131	Ballydermot	Sold or scrapped
☐	**C45**	7132	Derrygreenagh	
☐	**C46**	7133	Tionnsca	Sold or scrapped

(1) C39 was the Type 4 prototype. It is now dismantled at the Irish Steam Preservation Society, Stradbally, County Laois

(2) Dismantled and in use as a PW Trolley on the Cavan & Leitrim Railway, Dromod Station, County Leitrim

Wickham type
4S/BB railcar C43
at Blackwater,
County Offaly,
in July 1973.
Peter Nicholson

Wickham type
4S/BB railcar C45,
complete with
warning triangle,
at Esker on the
Clonsast system
in County Offaly,
on 15th May 1988.
Hamish Stevenson

Wickham type 4S/BB Mk.II railcar C58 at Blackwater, County Offaly, in July 1973. Peter Nicholson

BORD NA MÓNA / SOUTHERN MOTORS RAILCAR   4wPMR

Built:	1958	Engine:	Ford Petrol
Weight:	c.3 tons	Transmission:	4-speed gearbox, chain
Wheel Diameter:		Horsepower:	
Gauge:	3 ft	Seating:	8

Fleet No	Makers No	Allocation	Remarks
☐ **C47**	3	–	Preserved. See note (1)
☐ **C48**	4	Coolnagun	Out of use
☐ **C49**	5	Mountdillon	
☐ **C50**	6	Ballydermot	Dismantled
☐ **C51**	7	Blackwater	
☐ **C52**	8	Tionnsca	Dismantled
☐ **C53**	9	Derrygreenagh	Out of use
☐ **C54**	10	Blackwater	Dismantled

(1)   C47 is preserved on the Cavan & Leitrim Railway, Dromod Station, County Leitrim

WICKHAM TYPE 4S/BB (Mk.II †) RAILCAR   2w+2wPMR

Built:	1957, 1960†	Engine:	JAP 600cc petrol
Weight:		Transmission:	Mechanical
Wheel Diameter:		Horsepower:	
Gauge:	3 ft	Seating:	

Fleet No	Makers No	Allocation	Remarks
☐ **C55**	7680	Blackwater	Out of use
☐ **C56**	7681	–	See note (1)
☐ **C57**	7682	Coolnagan	Sold or scrapped
☐ **C58 †**	8630	Blackwater	Type 4S/BB Mk.II. Out of use
☐ **C59 †**	8631	Blackwater	Type 4S/BB Mk.II. Sold or scrapped

(1)   Stored by the Irish Narrow Gauge Trust at a private location in Cahir, County Tipperary

Bord na Móna 4wPMR railcar C60, at Mountdillon, County Longford, 19th July 1973. Peter Nicholson

BORD NA MÓNA RAILCAR

		4wPMR	
Built:	1960	Engine:	Turner, Ford *, MWM petrol †
Weight:		Transmission:	Mechanical
Wheel Diameter:		Horsepower:	
Gauge:	3 ft	Seating:	

Fleet No	Makers No	Allocation	Remarks
☐ **C60**	BnM	Mountdillon	Formerly No 1. See note (1). Sold or scrapped
☐ **C61†**	BnM	Littleton	Formerly No 1. See note (2). Dismantled
☐ **C62***	BnM	Mountdillon	Formerly No 2. See note (3)

(1) Built by Bord na Móna at Mountdillon Works
(2) Built by Bord na Móna at Littleton Works
(3) Built by Bord na Móna at Ballydermot Works

Bord na Móna 4wPMR railcar C68, crossing the lifting bridge over the Grand Canal, near Allenwood in County Kildare, on 9th May 1986. Hamish Stevenson

BORD NA MÓNA RAILCAR   4wPMR (2w+2wPMR‡)

Built:	1972	Engine:	4 Cylinder Petrol
Weight:		Transmission:	4 Speed Gearbox, Chain
Wheel Diameter:		Horsepower:	
Gauge:	3 ft	Seating:	

	Fleet No	Makers No	Allocation	Remarks
☐	**C63**	BnM	Attymon	Out of use
☐	**C64**	BnM	Littleton	Unmotorised. Dismantled
☐	**C65**	BnM	Mountdillon	
☐	**C66**	BnM	Kilberry	Out of use
☐	**C67**	BnM	Derrygreenagh	Out of use
☐	**C68**	BnM	Ballydermot	
☐	**C69**	BnM	Ballydermot	Out of use
☐	**C70**	BnM	Tionnsca	Out of use
☐	**C71**	BnM	Mountdillon	
☐	**C72**	BnM	Ballivor	
☐	**C73**	BnM	Coolnagun	Out of use
☐	**C74**	BnM	Boora	Formerly numbered 74. Out of use
☐	**C75**	BnM	Blackwater	
☐	**C76**	BnM	Derrygreenagh	Out of use
☐	**C77 ‡**	BnM	Coolnagun	Out of use
☐	**C78**	BnM	Boora	Unmotorised
☐	**C79**	BnM	Ballydermot	Out of use
☐	**C80**	BnM	Blackwater	Has a Morris engine. See inside back cover.

WICKHAM TYPE 14ST RAILCAR TRAILER   2w+2w

Built:	1949	Engine:	Unpowered
Gauge:	3 ft	Seating:	14

	Fleet No	Makers No	Allocation	Remarks
☐	–	4825	?	See notes to Railcars C31 and C32.

This former Cardiff bus has been converted to a carriage and is used for transporting occasional special school parties around the Mountdillon system, where it was photographed on 31st July 1995.

RAIL TRACTORS

Bord na Móna also have a small fleet of converted agricultural tractors. Most sit on a 4 wheel frame with the road wheels removed. The drive is by chain from the rear tractor axle to the wheelset beneath. They are equipped with oxy-acetyene welding gear, a vice and other tools for on site repairs. Some still carry their original road registration numbers.

Fleet No /Registration	Drive	Builder / Date	Allocation	Remarks
☐ **F 210**	2+2wDM	BnM	Littleton	
☐ **F 222**	2+2wDM	BnM / 1983	Blackwater.	Named *Bog Foreman*
☐ **F 230** / CIR 862	2+2wDM	BnM	Blackwater	
☐ **F 308**	2+2wDM	Massey Ferguson	Boora	
☐ **F 321**	2+2wDM	Massey Ferguson	Boora	
☐ **F 348**	2+2wDM	BnM	Blackwater	
☐ **F 349**	2+2wDM	BnM	Blackwater	
☐ **F 353**	2+2wDM	BnM / 1983	Blackwater	
☐ **F 360**	2+2wDM	BnM / 1983	Littleton	
☐ **F 630** / 341 NRI	2+2wDM	BnM	Blackwater	
☐ **F 635**	2+2wDM	BnM	Boora	
☐ **F 842** / CIR 861	2+2wDM	BnM	Blackwater	
☐ **F 851** / 726 XZ	2+2wDM	BnM	Blackwater	
☐ **F 866**	2+2wDM	BnM / c1975	Blackwater	
☐ **F 878**	2+2wDM	BnM / c1975	Blackwater	
☐ **?**	2+2wDM	BnM / c1975		

Bord na Móna rail tractor F353 at Blackwater, County Offaly, on 2nd August 1995.

OTHER ITEMS OF INTEREST

BLACKWATER WORKS MACHINERY MUSEUM, COUNTY OFFALY

On display here at the Bord na Móna Machinery Museum is a Ruston Hornsby LBT 4wDM locomotive. Formerly in use with the ESB at Portarlington, it did not see any service with Bord na Móna. Other details are as follows:

Built:	1954	Makers no:	422566
Weight:	3¼ tons	Engine:	Ruston 3VSH
Wheel Diameter:	1 ft 4⁵⁄₆ in	Transmission:	3-speed, chain
Gauge:	3 ft	Horsepower:	31½ hp at 1,200 rpm

CLONMACNOISE & WEST OFFALY RAILWAY

The undermentioned stock is based here, to take visitors on conducted tours around part of the extensive railway system, which focuses on Blackwater Works at Shannonbridge, in County Offaly.

Fleet No	Makers No	Remarks
☐ **LM 111**	379079	Ruston & Hornsby 40DL locomotive – see page 16.
☐ **LM 322**	8923	Hunslet Wagonmaster locomotive – see page 29.
☐ **LM 323**	8924	Hunslet Wagonmaster locomotive – see page 29.
☐ **TC 1**	–	Air conditioned 52 seat carriage for the Tourist Train, built 1992 by Metro Walker of Clara.
☐ **TC 2**	–	Air conditioned 52 seat carriage for the Tourist Train, built 1994 by J Mangan & Sons, Edenderry.
☐ –	3389	Passenger carriage section built at Inchicore Works in 1952 from former Walker Brothers railcar, ex-West Clare section of CIE. Out of use. On display at Blackwater. To move to Littleton, County Tipperary.

BELLACORICK BOG RAILWAY

The undermentioned stock is based here, to take visitors on conducted tours around part of the Oweninny complex of bogs at Bellacorick, in County Mayo.

Fleet No	Makers No	Allocation	Remarks
☐ **LM 123**	379925		Ruston & Hornsby 48DL locomotive. Used to haul the above carriage on the Bellacorick Bog Railway – see page 17.
☐ –	3386		Passenger carriage section built at Inchicore Works in 1952 from former Walker Brothers railcar used on the West Clare section of CIE. Used on Bellacorick Bog Railway at Oweninny.

We hope that you have enjoyed this Midland Publishing book.

Further titles are in the course of preparation. We welcome ideas on what you would like to see. If you have a manuscript or project that you think merits publication, we would be happy to consider it: but please send only brief details initially.

In addition, our associate company, Midland Counties Publications, offer an exceptionally wide range of books and videos for sale by mail-order around the world. For probably Europe's biggest range of titles in the fields of railways, aviation, buses & trams, tractors and commercial vehicles, naval & merchant shipping, militaria, astronomy and spaceflight, please write, telephone or fax for a copy of the appropriate catalogue to:

Midland Counties Publications, Unit 3 Maizefield, Hinckley, Leics., LE10 1YF
Teephonel: 01455 233 747 or Fax: 01455 233 737

TURF CO-OPERATIVES

As mentioned on page 6, three former Bord na Móna locations have become workers co-operatives in recent years. The locomotives and railcars at these locations retain their Bord na Móna numbers and have been listed at the appropriate point in the preceding pages. The stock at these locations is summarised below.

ATTYMON PEAT CO-OP SOCIETY LIMITED

Locomotives and railcars based at Attymon:
- [ ] LM 17 E
- [ ] LM 22
- [ ] LM 34
- [ ] LM 38 E
- [ ] LM 346
- [ ] C 63

Locomotives based at Clonkeen:
- [ ] LM 41 E
- [ ] LM 164 Q

THE COOLNAGUN PEAT COMPANY LIMITED, COOLNAGUN, CO. WESTMEATH

The following locomotives and railcars are leased from Bord na Móna:
- [ ] LM 35 E
- [ ] LM 50
- [ ] LM 51
- [ ] LM 70
- [ ] LM 89 J
- [ ] LM 172
- [ ] LM 341
- [ ] C 48
- [ ] C 57
- [ ] C 73
- [ ] C 77

GLENTIES TURF CO-OP SOCIETY, ADARA ROAD, GLENTIES, COUNTY DONEGAL

The following locomotives and railcars are leased from Bord na Móna:
- [ ] LM 20 A
- [ ] LM 26 E
- [ ] LM 198
- [ ] LM 263
- [ ] LM 264
- [ ] C 16

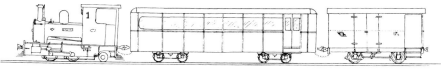

Clonmacnoise & West Offaly Railway

An opportunity to experience a five-and-a-half mile circular tour in a specially built coach on Bord na Móna's narrow gauge railway. It will show you Blackwater Bog – a major raised bog, and Bord na Móna's activities on it. You will also see conserved bog, a restored wetland and a Bord na Móna machinery museum.

Coffee shop, Craft shop, Large coach and car park, Picnic areas, Field project area.

Open: 1st April to 31st October.

Trains leave every hour on the hour, 10.00 to 17.00 (inclusive). Special trains arranged on demand all year round, by advance arrangement, eg Nature Trails, Railway Enthusiasts.

Prices: Adult £3.25 Child £2.25 Family £8.50 (1996) Group rate also available.

Location: off N62, near Ballinasloe

Bord na Móna, Blackwater / Uisce Dubh Shannonbridge, Athlone, Co Westmeath

Telephone: +353 905 74114 / 74172 / 74121 Fax: +353 905 74210

BELLACORICK BOG TRAIN

A guided tour on this Bord na Móna narrow gauge railway, using refurbished carriages of the West Clare Railway.

See Ireland's first Windfarm; the wonders of Blanket Bog; traditional hand-won turf; modern peat harvesting; beautiful landscapes.

R&H 48DL LM123 at Bellacorick, August 1995.

Open: 1st May to 30th September.

Prices: Adult £3.00 Students/OAPs £1.75 Family £8.00 (1996)

Location: North Mayo, between Crossmolina and Bangor (route N59)

Bord na Móna, Bellacorick, Co Mayo

Further details: Telephone: +353 96 53002 Fax: +353 96 53094

29/11/03